World Issues

CONSUMERISM

Alex Woolf

Chrysalis Children's Books

WORLD ISSUES

ABORTION   EQUAL OPPORTUNITIES   HUMAN RIGHTS
ANIMAL RIGHTS   EUTHANASIA   POVERTY
ARMS TRADE   FOOD TECHNOLOGY   RACISM
CAPITAL PUNISHMENT   GENETIC ENGINEERING   REFUGEES
CONSUMERISM   GENOCIDE   TERRORISM
DRUGS

First published in the UK in 2004 by
(*) Chrysalis Children's Books
An imprint of Chrysalis Books Group Plc
The Chrysalis Building, Bramley Road, London W10 6SP

Editorial Manager: Joyce Bentley
Editor: Clare Lewis
Project Editor: Jon Richards
Designer: Ed Simkins
Picture Researcher: Lorna Ainger
Educational Consultant: Lizzy Bacon

Produced by Tall Tree Ltd

ISBN: 1 84458 078 4

British Library Cataloguing in Publication Data for this book is available from the British Library.
Printed in Hong Kong

10 9 8 7 6 5 4 3 2 1

Picture Acknowledgments
The publishers would like to thank the following for their permission to reproduce the photographs:
The Advertising Archive Ltd: 25
Alamy Images: Gina Calvi 9c, Vintage Images 13
Art Archive: Bibliothèque des Arts Décoratifs Paris/Dagli Orti 19, Bodleian Library Oxford 15, Musée Guimet Paris/Dagli Orti 12
Corbis: H Armstrong Roberts 44, John B Boykin 36, Henry Diltz 40, Robert Essel NYC 21, Nick Gunderson 20, Dave G. Houser 28, Jacques Langevin/Sygma 34, Lester Lefkowitz 11, Richard T Nowitz 43, Fridman Paulo/Sygma 10, Les Stone/Sygma 7, 42, Peter Turnley 49
Getty Images: Natalie Behring-Chisholm 31, Gerd George 22, Eric Larrayadieu 5, 26, Oleg Nikishin 32, Michel Porro 14, Gary M. Prior 24, Alex Wong 23
ImageState: 27
PA Photos: 18, EPA 9b, 33, 37, 39, 41, 45, 47, 50, Pana-jij photos 17, Chris Young 16
Jon Richards: 30, 46
Still Pictures: Mark Edwards 9t, 48, Russell Gordon 29, Olivier Langrand 38, Hartmut Schwarzbach 8, Charlotte Thege 35

CONTENTS

Rajendra's Story

*We buy all sorts of products every day, but we rarely stop
to think about how those products reached the shops, or
what hidden costs they might contain. The following
story is about someone working in India's carpet
industry. The carpets he works on are sold to shops in
Europe and the United States. One of them may have
even ended up on your floor...*

RAJENDRA IS FOURTEEN. He is a carpet weaver in Uttar
Pradesh in northeastern India. He works on a loom for 15
hours a day, seven days a week, with only a short break for
lunch. For this he is paid 10 rupees (13 pence) per day by the
loom owner. At noon he is given two roti (pieces of bread)
with salt, and the same again when he stops work in the
evening. The loom is in a small, poorly lit, village hut,
with tiny, heavily barred windows.

Rajendra has worked here for three years. His
father, Bhagwan, was too poor to take care of his
large family, and went to the loom owner for a
loan. In return, Rajendra was forced to work
for the loom owner. In the early days, he
would make mistakes, or would work too
slowly. For this, the loom owner would
beat him with a bamboo stick.

Rajendra's eyesight is poor, he has a lung disease from inhaling wool particles, and he is bent-backed from spending such long hours at the loom. Lack of nutritious food has made him small for his age.

Rajendra is just one of 300 000 children who weave carpets in India. Most of them live and work in appalling conditions, and yet they are part of a very profitable industry: Indian carpet exports earn around £400 million per year; over a third of these carpets are sold in the USA.

The Costs of Consumerism

Consumerism affects all parts of the world, both human and natural, in many different ways.

BRAZIL
In Brazil, the growing worldwide demand for beef has meant the destruction of rainforests to clear land for pastures. This has caused a loss of fertile topsoil and a severe reduction in the water supply, because of the water needed for cattle and to grow their feed.

INDONESIA
Since 1990, the Indonesian paper industry has experienced rapid expansion. To supply their mills, producers have seized large areas of land for their plantations. Many locals, who depended on this land for farming, have lost their livelihoods.

CHINA
Chinese-made shoes are sold all over the world. However, customers may not be aware that the workers in these Chinese shoe factories are regularly required to work 16 hours a day, seven days a week, and that drops in production can lead to brutal punishments.

What Is Consumerism?

People have always had basic needs, such as for food, clothing and shelter. As societies grew wealthier, however, people's appetites changed. They became interested in acquiring things for reasons other than mere survival. This is what consumerism is. It is an attitude that values the purchase of goods that are desirable, but not essential.

IN A CONSUMERIST society, people become caught up in the process of shopping, and take part of their identity from the new items they buy. They take care over the clothes and cars and household furnishings they purchase, because these things form part of an image they wish to project about themselves.

Just as consumerism is driven by the consumers' desire for luxury goods, so it is also driven by the producers' desire for profits. On the production side, a number of industries are used both to serve and encourage consumerism. Researchers develop new products to tempt consumers; designers try to find fresh ways to make products attractive;

DEBATE – Is the 24-hour society a good thing?

- Yes. It gives people flexibility over when they can shop.
- No. It is unfair on employees who have to work at unsociable hours.

Today, supermarkets have expanded the range of goods they sell beyond just foodstuffs, and some offer clothes, books, banking services and even cars!

These neon adverts reflect the desire of companies to push their products 24 hours a day, even after most people have gone to bed!

advertisers try to bring these products and services to the attention of the public; and retailers try their best to lure customers into their shops.

What are the main effects?

Consumerism has affected society in many ways – some good, some bad. It has led to a breakdown of traditional class divisions, as people of all social backgrounds have gained access to a wide range of luxury goods. On the other hand, it has given rise to greater divisions between rich and poor, because producers have exploited labourers in poorer countries, who work for less money than those in richer countries, in order to increase their profits. Consumerism has also taken its toll on the environment, with expanding demand leading to an unsustainable use of natural resources.

The 24-hour society

Modern consumers expect a wider choice of products and services, as well as the freedom to buy these when they wish. As a result, the world is fast becoming a 24-hour society, where goods can be purchased at any time of the day or night. Many shops are now open from 7am until 11pm, and some supermarkets are open for 24 hours a day almost every day of the week. Over the telephone or the Internet, holidays, books, food, banking and legal services can be purchased at all times, 365 days a year. This allows people to do their shopping at a time that suits them. The 24-hour society has also changed the world of work, with more people working longer or more flexible hours, rather than the traditional nine-to-five.

Has Consumerism Always Existed?

Consumerism has its origins in ancient times. In the first century BC, noble-born Romans acquired a taste for luxury products, such as silk from China. By the 13th century, the European aristocracy had become interested in clothing, objects and spices from the Far East. Possession of these was often used to display a person's wealth and status – a key aspect of consumerism.

HOWEVER, UNLIKE TODAY, these early forms of consumerism only affected a small, wealthy minority. Most people in ancient and medieval societies were too poor to develop consumerist urges. Much of their trade was based on exchanging goods and services, rather than buying them with money, so there was little cash available to buy luxury products. There is also evidence to suggest that in medieval times, people were often deterred from acquiring unnecessary products because of their religious beliefs. Christianity and Buddhism, in particular, stressed that worldly possessions made it harder to achieve spiritual salvation.

When did modern consumerism begin?

Consumerism in its modern form first emerged in Western Europe in the late 17th century. By this time, a middle class of business people, merchants and professionals had established itself.

A statue showing a Chinese woman from the Tang dynasty (AD 618–907) wearing a tall hat that was fashionable for the period.

A smaller version of the umbrella, called the parasol, became an important part of a woman's outfit in the 18th and 19th centuries. It was used to shade the carrier's face from the sun.

The umbrella

A classic early consumer product, the umbrella was first used by the ancient Egyptians and Romans to shelter them from the weather. During the Middle Ages, however, umbrellas were regarded as something of a novelty and their use declined. Then at some point in the 17th century, Europeans decided that they disliked getting wet – something that had never bothered them much before. French nobles began using umbrellas, having borrowed the idea from the Chinese, and their usage gradually filtered down through society. The fashion reached rainy England in the 1770s, where they were criticised at first for being unmanly and foreign. However, they soon caught on, and are now very much a part of the English identity.

Colonies were being set up in the Americas and the Far East, giving this class of wealthy Europeans access to many exotic products. Early consumer favourites included sugar and coffee from the Americas, tea and porcelain from China, spices from Southeast Asia and cotton from India.

In the 18th century, new ways of marketing and selling goods were developed. Shopkeepers began enticing customers into their stores with window displays or the offer of discounts and bargains. Advertisements filled the newspapers that began appearing in cities. Consumers became susceptible to fads and fashions. For example, in the early 1700s, there was a craze for tall hats, wigs and wide skirts for women. By the end of the century, people became more conscious of body odour, causing a boom in perfume sales for both sexes. The patterns of buying and selling that were established in the 18th century continue to this day.

How did consumerism develop?

The next big development in consumerism came with the arrival of the department store. The first one opened in Paris in the 1830s, and the idea quickly spread to the major cities in Europe and North America. Consumers were now faced with a vast range of products, attractively displayed, in spacious surroundings. Department stores were visited as much for the pleasure of the experience as for the act of purchasing. Browsing became a popular pastime, and shopping was transformed into a leisure activity. Another 19th-century innovation was the catalogue, which allowed rural and small-town dwellers to buy from the major stores by ordering goods that could be sent by mail.

What has changed since 1900?

In the early 20th century, manufacturers of long-lasting consumer products, such as cars, faced the problem that their customers would only buy from them occasionally. They solved this by introducing 'planned obsolescence' to their products. By bringing out a new range of products each year, they could persuade customers that what they bought the previous year was now out of date.

In the 20th century, technological advances made it possible to create new products, including artificial fabrics like nylon, music systems and computers. New means of advertising and selling were made possible by the development of radio in the 1920s, television in the 1950s and the Internet in the 1990s.

Tulips became a novelty purchase and then a genuine passion, particularly in the Netherlands, in the 1630s. In some cases, tulip bulbs would change hands for a small fortune.

Consumerist leisure

One of the biggest growth areas in the 20th century was leisure. People were increasingly inclined to spend their money on being entertained. Sports, such as baseball in the USA, became major leisure activities, spawning a new industry of sports equipment manufacturers. Amusement parks arrived in the 1890s with the invention of the ferris wheel and roller coaster. The first movies were shown around 1900, and by 1920, families were seeing a movie every week. In consumerist leisure – as in all forms of consumerism – the latest thing was always the most popular, and fashions in entertainment changed regularly.

Consumerism also spread to many different activities in the 20th century. In the 1920s and 1930s, eating out became popular with the opening of fish and chip shops in the UK and hamburger restaurants in the United States. Consumerism affected transport with the invention of the bicycle and then the car. With the development of the aeroplane, holidays abroad became another major consumer purchase. Today, almost every major field of human activity has been affected by consumerism, including religious festivals, weddings and child-rearing.

DEBATE – Was the rise of consumerism inevitable?

- Yes. The desire for material comforts is a natural urge.
- No. Consumerism came about due to the development of mass-production techniques and the consequent need for producers to sell more goods.

A 19th-century advert for a popular beef extract, first introduced in 1874. In this example, humour was used to appeal to its target audience of housewives.

What Drives Us To Consume?

Is consumerism an inevitable consequence of human nature, or is it the result of historical developments? The answer is probably a bit of both. Social changes from the 16th century onward laid the foundations for consumerism. However, the growth of consumerism today suggests that it appeals to something in our nature, such as our desire for comfort and status.

FROM THE 16TH CENTURY, the European economy expanded rapidly, bringing vast profits to merchants and manufacturers. This new spending power, coupled with a desire to imitate social superiors, encouraged consumerism. The Church, with its emphasis on simple living, had declined in power by the 18th century. A new philosophy emerged, known as the

How do businesses create demand?

Appreciate the following line of reasoning: 'I can imagine it, therefore I want it. I want it, therefore I should have it. Because I should have it, I need it. Because I need it, I deserve it. Because I deserve it, I will do anything necessary to get it.' This is the artificial internal drive that the advertisers tap into. You 'can imagine it' because they will bombard your consciousness with its image until you move to step two, 'I want it... etc.' This is one of the things that allows people to surrender to consumerism.

Source: *Overcoming Consumerism*, an anti-consumerism website

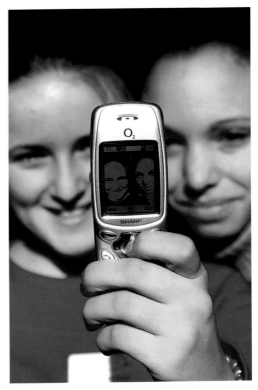

Picture phones were introduced in the UK in 2002, but it was another year before the idea took off. By clever marketing, a luxury good such as this has been turned into a must-have item.

Enlightenment, which stressed improving our lives on Earth through the use of reason and science, rather than preparing our souls for heaven; spending money on luxury goods became acceptable behaviour.

In the 19th century, the Romance movement of writers and artists praised physical beauty. People were inspired to buy clothes and products that enhanced their own beauty and that of their homes. In the 20th century, one of the driving forces behind consumerism was the breakdown of class divisions,

leading to a greater emphasis on status symbols, such as expensive houses, clothes or cars.

Today, increased stress or boredom in personal and professional lives lead many to seek comfort or excitement in shopping. This is often the case with lower-middle-class people, such as secretaries and sales personnel, whose jobs involve a lot of routine. For example, in Germany between 1900 and 1930, the lower middle classes led in movie-going, the purchase of radios and cigarette smoking.

Shopping has become a popular way to relax and have fun for people of all ages.

Product placement

In the 1982 film, *ET*, a sweet called Reese's Pieces appeared in an important scene, causing sales of this product to jump by 65 per cent. Ever since then, product placement – the inclusion of products in movies, on TV and even in video games – has become a significant promotional technique. Interactive TV will allow viewers to order a featured product – for example a shirt being worn by a TV star – simply by clicking on it. Digital advertising uses computer technology to insert products into scenes that were never there to begin with. This is most commonly seen in televised sporting events, where adverts are projected onto billboards or playing surfaces in stadiums.

Why do businesses advertise?

Advertisements are used by businesses to promote their products. The growth in the number of adverts we see around us is a reflection of the power of consumerism in today's world.

Early adverts tended to be wordy descriptions of products in newspapers. Then, in the late 19th century, as colour printing became cheaper, the nature of advertising changed. Instead of using words to describe the product, advertisers aimed to make a visual impact: colourful posters appeared containing attractive images and few words, designed to appeal to people's emotions rather than their reason.

The first advertising agencies were founded in New York City in 1870, and from this point on promoting and selling goods became a more sophisticated and professional process. Today, companies spend a great deal of time researching their customers' desires and aspirations.

COMETH THE HOUR.

Roadside advertisers have just seconds to convey their message, so they use very few words and instantly recognisable images.

This late 19th-century French poster uses few words and makes its impact with an eye-catching picture.

They then use this information as a basis for their advertisements. For example, a motor manufacturer aiming to sell a car to 20-somethings might emphasise the speed and power of their vehicles; whereas the same company trying to sell a different model to an older age group might prefer to stress the car's safety features and roomy interior.

Has consumerism affected advertising?

The evidence of consumerism is all around us in the sheer number of adverts that we see in our daily lives. Adverts are everywhere: as well as the usual places, they now appear on petrol pumps, lavatory stalls, elevator walls, park benches, telephone kiosks, bus and train tickets and even on space rockets. It has been estimated that we see up to 3000 adverts per day.

Sporting events, stadiums, museums, parks, schools, theatres and universities are now often named after their sponsors. People have become walking advertisements, with designer labels visible on their jeans and shirts. Celebrities are increasingly used to endorse products by being seen to use and wear them in public appearances, and even promoting them in interviews. Consumerism, in the form of adverts, has become a highly visible part of our daily landscape.

DEBATE – Do adverts manipulate people into buying more than they need?

- Yes. Adverts operate on the subconscious level, so that we are mostly unaware of their effect on our buying decisions.

- No. Adverts may be more sophisticated than they were, but essentially do the job they have always done: promoting products. The choice to buy, as ever, remains with the consumer.

How Does Consumerism Affect Society?

Consumerism has changed society in many different ways. The range and accessibility of products now on offer have served to make life more convenient and stimulating. However, the temptations of consumerism have also caused problems for some. For example, families have been led into debt, health problems are on the increase and so is shoplifting.

Shopping malls are now found in almost every major Western town and city. The world's largest, in Edmonton, Canada, has more than 800 stores.

BUSINESSES HAVE found ingenious ways to make shopping a quicker, more convenient and more pleasurable experience. Today, the department store has increasingly given way to the mall, a vast sprawl of shops

Shoplifting

The intense desires and frustrations that consumer culture can provoke in people are partly to blame for a steep increase in shoplifting. In the USA, there are approximately 23 million shoplifters (one out of every 11 Americans) stealing around US$25 million worth of goods per day. Personal and social pressures may be the main cause of this behaviour, but it is a sign of our consumerist times that people choose to relieve these pressures by stealing goods from shops.

in an enclosed area. With shops, restaurants and entertainment venues now located in the same place, shopping has become even more associated with leisure. For those with even less time on their hands, the Internet and interactive TV allow shopping to be done at the shopper's own convenience.

What are some of the negative effects of consumerism?

Not all the social effects of consumerism are beneficial, however. With so many more must-have products around for the fashion- or status-conscious, consumer spending is rising as a proportion of people's income, leading many families into debt. By 2001, over half of all Americans had almost no savings because of the amount they were spending on products and services, while a third were living from paycheque to paycheque, and were often heavily in debt. This problem has been made worse by the way some banks and loan companies encourage people to borrow money on their credit cards.

Consumerism can also be blamed for other social ills. The heavy marketing of delicious but unhealthy foods, such as sweets, soft drinks, crisps, burgers and fries, has caused a significant rise in diet-related health problems, especially obesity. In the 1990s, for the first time in human history, the world's population of overweight people was roughly the same as the number of underfed people, at about 1.1 billion. In the USA, 55 per cent of adults are overweight, and 23 per cent are obese, according to international standards. In the UK, 35 per cent of people are affected by diet-related diseases such as cardiovascular disease, cancer, diabetes and malnutrition.

Consumerism has now invaded almost every aspect of human society, including traditional cultures, as illustrated by these two Australian Aboriginal children using a laptop computer.

Consumerism and romance

Consumerist attitudes are so entrenched in society that they even affect how people conduct their relationships. Take romance, for example. The concept of 'dating' began around 1910, and the key difference between this and earlier forms of courtship was the involvement of some consumerist activity, such as a movie or a restaurant. Young men and women came to judge their dates in consumerist terms: for instance, how generous was one partner to another? If an engagement followed, an expensive ring would often be expected. As for the wedding, there are now a range of services available for the special day, including flowers, catering, music, photographs and videos.

What other activities has consumerism affected?

The effects of consumerism are not just limited to the way that we shop. Consumerism has spread to a number of other activities, such as holidays and celebrations. People have been buying Christmas presents since the 1830s, and by the end of the 19th century, Christmas shopping had become a huge commercial event. This remains the case today: in the week before Christmas 2002, American shoppers spent about US$145 billion, compared to around US$80 billion per week during the rest of the year.

The idea of celebrating birthdays with gift-giving was another 19th-century invention. The first commercial Valentine cards were sold in Britain in 1855, and Mother's Day cards followed in 1914. Festivals and celebrations have increasingly become a vehicle to sell more products, and this has threatened to obscure the original meanings of these events.

Many couples now spend a lot of money on Valentine's Day by giving each other presents or by going out for 'romantic' meals.

Museums, art galleries and other tourist sites have adopted a consumerist attitude with increasing space given over to shops selling souvenirs. In 2000, Americans spent US$1.5 billion on souvenirs.

Has consumerism affected life outside shopping?

Consumerist attitudes have also spread to politics. Today, political parties approach marketing companies to coordinate their election campaigns. Political candidates are sold like consumer products, adjusting their voice and appearance, their slogans and sometimes even their policies, to maximise their appeal to the electorate.

Many universities are becoming more commercial in their attitudes, especially in the USA. Students and parents are often treated like customers. Courses and professors are rated for their quality and the results achieved. The demand for good results has led to a rise in grade levels without any corresponding increase in the quality of work.

Consumerism has also affected sport in a big way. Sportspeople now compete not simply to win, but to get rich. The most successful can earn millions from prize money and sponsorships. Businesses, eager to associate themselves with sporting heroes, are happy to pay them generously to promote their products. The temptations of sponsorship have been blamed for leading some athletes to take performance-enhancing drugs.

David Beckham has come to symbolise the changing views of men and women in consumerism. He is portrayed as a man who is interested in fashion and looking good and has been used to sell fashion and beauty products.

Madam CJ Walker

In the early 20th century, African-American women found it hard to participate in the consumerism enjoyed by their white compatriots. They were not welcomed in many stores because of racial discrimination, and there were few beauty products designed specifically for them. The situation started to change with the arrival of Madam CJ Walker, who invented a hair-care formula for black women in the early 1900s. Unable to sell her product in the shops, she began selling it door-to-door. She soon established a highly successful system of training, distribution and marketing across the Southern and Midwestern states of the USA. The sales agents and hairdressers she trained went on to train others, eventually widening distribution throughout the nation. Having started out – so she said – with half a dollar in her pocket, Walker's company achieved sales of US$500 000 in 1919, the year she died.

Are men and women different kinds of consumers?

Until the 18th century, most consumers were men, and products were directed almost exclusively at them. However, the 18th century witnessed a new interest in household items such as implements for cooking, dining and cleaning – areas traditionally under women's control. This raised the status of women as consumers.

From the early 19th century, men became less inclined to beautify themselves, and women began to lead the way in consumption of clothing and beauty products. In the 1890s, women's magazines started to appear, such as *Ladies' Home Journal*, *Woman's Home Companion* and *Good Housekeeping*, with pictures of the latest fashions, along with recipes and housekeeping tips.

By the 1910s, many young women entered the labour market, and for the first time enjoyed direct access to their own money – an advantage they were unlikely to give up once they were married. Women started to become the dominant group of consumers of food, clothing and other everyday household goods.

What other products appealed to women?

In the 1920s, they even began trespassing on previously male-dominated areas such as cigarette smoking, alcohol and cars. Advertisers were quick to see this trend and began to produce advertisements that promoted aspects of their products that were seen to be of interest to women; car adverts from this period, for example, began to focus on the product's colour, ease-of-use, design and upholstery.

Since the 1980s, men have begun to show the same interest in appearance-enhancing products as women. This has been revealed in the increasing number of men's fashion magazines, hair dyes and cosmetics on the market. Men are also now rivalling women in their interest in cosmetic surgery. Sports retailers currently give far more floor and shelf space to fashion-related products than sports equipment.

Punch, May 14 1958

"I know the secret of learning to drive . . .

it's as simple as A.B.C. when there's only two pedals to concentrate on"

Suit by Frederick Starke. Hat by Otto Lucas, London

Maybe you can't drive *now*, but you can easily learn in a car fitted with MANUMATIC. This simple 2-pedal system completely disposes of the clutch pedal—and all the problems that go with it. Make sure your next car is a real *family* car that you can drive as well as your husband. Make sure it's fitted with MANUMATIC!

The Selective-Automatic
manumatic
REGD TRADE MARK
2 *Pedal motoring at its best!*
Send for this full colour catalogue which describes the joys of 2-pedal motoring.
AVAILABLE ON:
AUSTIN A55 · HILLMAN MINX · M.G. MAGNETTE · MORRIS OXFORD · WOLSELEY 15/50
DEPT. P. AUTOMOTIVE PRODUCTS CO. LTD. LEAMINGTON SPA WARWICKSHIRE   M17

Whereas previous car advertisements focussed on aspects of cars that appealed to men, such as speed, performance and reliability, advertisements aimed at women were designed to appeal to more 'feminine' attributes. In this case, the manufacturer has chosen to point out how much easier it is to use two pedals instead of the usual three.

Spokescharacters

During the 1980s, children's toy adverts increasingly used well-known cartoon characters to sell products. It was noticed that this could boost sales. The owners of the characters were happy to license them for this kind of use, and by 1987, 70 per cent of toy adverts used a 'spokescharacter'. The key to the success of this strategy is to ensure that the character is instantly recognisable to children. This is done by introducing the character to very young children through decorations, toys and television. Today, this has led to all sorts of cross-promotion of products, with cartoon characters promoting products on TV, in magazines and in fast-food restaurants.

Are children affected by consumerism?

In the 18th century, products aimed directly at children began appearing, such as toys, games and books. However, it was not until the 20th century that children became major consumers in their own right, with the ability to buy items for themselves, or to persuade their parents to buy things for them. Today, children are often conditioned from an early age in the principles of consumerism. A major cause of sibling rivalry is resentment that a brother or sister has a new toy. If children are upset, their parents may try to win back their good mood by buying them a treat.

There is now a huge range of children's products – from crisps and sweets to athletic shoes and video games. Manufacturers and retailers are adept at packaging these items in bright colours so that they catch the eye of children, and at placing these goods on the lower shelves of their stores, so that they are at children's eye level, and within easy

Supermarkets aim to tempt children by placing products such as toys, videos, sweets and crisps on the lower shelves.

Children playing a video game. Commercials showing children having fun using products such as video games can convey several messages, such as 'this product is cool' and 'you are inferior if you do not have this product'.

reach of their hands. It is assumed that if a child touches a product then there is at least a chance that his or her parents will buy it.

Why are children good consumers?

Children are in many ways the ideal consumers, being more susceptible than adults to changes in style and fashion, and providing a ready market for the latest crazes. As a result, a huge amount of money (US$2 billion every year in the USA alone) is spent on advertising to children, and in 1997, children's direct influence on parental purchases in the USA was estimated at US$188 billion (as opposed to US$5 billion in the 1960s).

Television advertising is seen as a major reason for the rise in children's consumerism. It is estimated, in Western countries, that children aged between two and 17 watch between 15 000 and 18 000 hours of television, compared to just 12 000 hours spent in school.

DEBATE – Should adverts be directed at children?

- Yes. Children have a right to learn about what products are being offered to them. If parents do not want to buy a product for their child, they do not have to.

- No. Young children are not able to distinguish between their needs and wants, and advertisers should not exploit this. Adverts place extra pressure on parents that they should not have to deal with.

The European Union is considering regulating advertising aimed at children, and in 1991, the Scandanavian country of Sweden banned advertisements from primetime children's television programmes. This decision was taken after research showed that children under ten were unable to tell the difference between a commercial and a programme.

How Does Consumerism Affect Poorer Countries?

So far we have looked at the effects of consumerism on the richer, Western nations. Far more damaging has been its economic and social impact on the poorer countries of the world.

CONSUMERISM encourages people in developed countries to expect ever more choice and availability in the range of products in their shops, including products made in many different parts of the world. Products that were once considered luxuries – such as coffee, tea, chocolate, and tobacco – are now commonplace items in every supermarket. These products grow in tropical and sub-tropical regions; they are low-priced because of mass-production techniques, and because land and labour in these areas is relatively cheap.

Large tracts of land in these countries have been bought up by Western corporations and turned over exclusively to growing 'cash crops' as they are called, much of it for export to the West. Poorer nations often become overly dependent on one crop, and a dip in world demand can have devastating consequences for their economy. As the major employers in these countries, multinational companies can dictate wages and land use. In many cases, the best agricultural land – which could be used to grow food for the local people –

A shanty town in Brazil. Such places have little access to clean water and sanitation, and people living here are prone to diseases such as cholera and typhoid.

Although the production of tobacco products is labour intensive, companies are able to keep their costs down by using cheap labour from poorer countries.

is turned over to non-food products like tobacco and flowers, for export.

The mechanised nature of mass farming has meant there is less work for rural workers. Hunger and poverty has driven many to the cities in search of jobs, creating slums and shanty towns on city outskirts, and consequent health problems. In Latin America and the Caribbean, 74 per cent of poor people live in these slum areas.

The beef trade

The rise of fast-food restaurants since the 1950s has turned beef into a major consumer product. The biggest fast-food chain, McDonald's, now has about 28 000 restaurants worldwide and is America's largest purchaser of beef. To satisfy worldwide demand for this product, millions of hectares in Latin America have been given over to pasture for cattle, or to grow grain for cattle feed. In Brazil, this has left some 4.8 million rural families landless.

How do companies influence governments?

Today, most multinational companies contract out the production of their goods to businesses in developing countries, where labour is cheap. For example, in 2001, the clothing manufacturer Gap Inc bought its goods from 3600 factories based in 50 countries around the world.

Because they do not actually own these businesses, multinational companies can easily switch production to other countries if economic conditions are more favourable there. This gives them a great deal of power over governments, who are eager to keep jobs in their countries. They sometimes use this power to influence government policy. For example, the Gambian government was forced to abolish certain restrictions on developing the tourist industry following pressure from multinationals.

What are the hidden costs of coffee?

Coffee is one of the major consumer products of the modern world. Upmarket coffee-shop chains such as Costa, Starbucks and Caffe Nero are commonplace on city high streets, selling a wide variety of coffees with names that have now entered the general vocabulary, such as 'caramel macchiato' and 'white chocolate mocha'. Starbucks alone had 10 000 outlets worldwide in 2003.

Coffee suffering

'The [coffee] companies know there is terrible suffering at the heart of their business, yet they do virtually nothing to help. [It is time] to shame them and change them.'

Source: Adrian Lovett, Oxfam

The instant variety of coffee is even more popular. Every second of the day, an estimated 3900 cups of Nescafé, the world's leading instant coffee brand, are drunk in 120 countries around the globe. Yet the coffee business is also an example of the dark side of consumerism, where greed for profits has left farmers in the producer nations in dire poverty.

The world's four biggest coffee companies are Kraft, Sara Lee, Proctor & Gamble and Nestlé. Each owns coffee brands worth over a billion dollars, yet coffee farmers receive just five per cent of the price consumers pay. Since 1992, coffee production has increased twice as fast as coffee consumption, leading to millions of bags of unused coffee in warehouses around the world. All this excess has driven prices down. The big four coffee companies have tried to limit the impact on their profits of coffee's low

Coffee shop chains such as Starbucks are making huge profits as the price of their main raw material slumps.

price by buying coffee as cheaply as possible. In 1997, when the currency of Vietnam lost its value, the multinationals took advantage of the cheap prices and began buying their coffee from Vietnam. This forced traditional growers in Africa and Central America to reduce their prices too. As a result, the price of coffee dropped by 50 per cent between 2000 and 2003, hitting a 30-year low.

How did this price fall affect farmers?

It left millions of coffee farmers around the world in situations close to starvation. Countries like Uganda, Ethiopia and Rwanda, which depend on coffee for half their export revenue, face economic collapse. The number of Ethiopians in need of emergency food aid has risen from six million to around 15 million, partly as a result of this crisis. Some farmers in South and Central America are so desperate they are switching from growing coffee to growing coca, the raw material for cocaine. Others are migrating to the cities in search of work.

Coffee-shop chains like Starbucks and Costa tend to pay fairer prices to coffee growers, but their contribution is not sufficient to lift farmers out of poverty.

DEBATE – Are consumers to blame if producers exploit their workers?

- Yes. If they refused to buy their products, producers would be forced to change their ways.
- No. Producers should take responsibility for treating their workers well, if necessary under pressure from governments.

A worker on a coffee plantation in Ethiopia where a large proportion of the population depend on the income from this one product.

Are Non-Western Countries Consumerist?

Consumerism began in the West, and Western countries remain the biggest consumers by far. Nevertheless, over the past 50 years, consumerism has had a strong influence on countries outside Western Europe and the United States, where it is associated with Western – particularly American – culture.

Since the collapse of communism in the Soviet Union in 1991, some Russians have become extremely rich and able to buy a wide range of luxury goods.

FOR MOST OF the 20th century, Russia formed the major territory of the Soviet Union, a communist country in which the state controlled all industry, and Western-style consumerism was almost unheard of. When the Soviet Union collapsed in 1991, the new government introduced a free-market capitalist system, similar to the one that operates in the West. Russian businesspeople, known as 'new Russians', grew very rich, and began to use their newly earned wealth to indulge in consumerist purchases.

The Russian economy struggled during the 1990s, however, and large parts of Russian society remained too poor to participate in consumerism. Others felt resentful of the showy displays of the new Russians, and some were even nostalgic for the days of the Soviet Union. Today, consumerism remains confined to a fairly narrow band of Russian society.

How consumerist is Japan?

Many East Asian countries have been eager to embrace the consumerism of the West, especially Japan – the most Americanised of non-Western countries.

When Disney World Japan, opened in 1984, the Japanese owners copied the original theme park in Los Angeles as closely as possible – including park areas such as Frontierland (which was renamed Westernland) and characters such as Mickey Mouse, who is very familiar to most Japanese children. By 1988, the theme park was attracting 13 million tourists every year, making it one of the most popular attractions in the whole country.

Gift giving is important in Japanese culture, and so the gift shops located on Disney World Japan's Main Street are particularly busy. For similar reasons, the festival of Christmas (in its modern, commercial form) is extremely popular in Japan, even though it is not a Christian country.

The Japanese are also frequently among the first to take up new technologies. For example, picture phones were launched there in 2001, before they were launched in Europe, and, by 2003, they had become an established part of Japanese youth culture.

Consumerism in China

Despite having a communist government, China has, since 1978, been moving towards a free-market economy, and the Chinese have displayed a huge appetite for consumerism. There has been a boom in electronic goods, cars and adverts. Also, the Chinese government has introduced a strict one-child-per-family policy in an effort to control the rapidly growing population, and this may have led parents to over-indulge their children.

Minnie Mouse greets the crowds at Disney World Japan.

How has the Islamic Middle East reacted to consumerism?

In the West, the rise of consumerism was helped by a decline in Christian belief. In the Middle East, however, the religion of Islam remains a powerful influence in the day-to-day lives of millions of people, and this has acted as a severe brake on the development of a consumer culture. The governments, and large portions of the population in these countries, regard the Western lifestyle as decadent and corrupt. Drinking alcohol and gambling, for example, are against Islamic law, and many Muslims believe that women should cover themselves in public. They are also shocked by the sexual and violent nature of many of today's Hollywood movies.

Despite these attitudes, consumerism has penetrated some Islamic societies. Turkey and Egypt both have a sizeable urban middle class, that enjoys spending money on consumer goods – both locally produced and imported. During the 1990s, for example, Turks were buying around 200 000 new cars every year. Even in very strict Islamic countries, such as Saudi Arabia, consumerism has had some impact.

DEBATE - Should Western companies try to push their products in non-Western countries.

- Yes. Companies have a right to seek new markets.
- No. Western products and advertising can erode local cultures, as young people increasingly adopt Western diet, clothing, art and music.

A Muslim woman, dressed in a traditional Burka, shops for jewellery in a Western-style store in Dhahran, Saudi Arabia.

Global brands like this one are now advertised and sold in almost every country of the world.

جعل من كل اللحظات

Oil revenues have made certain sections of Saudi society very rich, and some people enjoy spending their money on luxury cars and shopping sprees in Western cities.

What happened in Iran?

During the 1970s, there was a surge of consumerism in Iran. This was boosted by television, which had attracted 15 million viewers, or half the population. Commercials promoted clothing and cosmetics, and many young Iranians were attracted by the Western lifestyle as depicted in TV programmes, soaps and movies imported from the USA. This era of consumerism in Iran was brief, however, and was brought to a sudden end with the Islamic revolution of 1979 (see pages 42–43).

African consumerism

The reaction of African countries to consumerism has been mixed. Some have been eager to adopt Western lifestyles, while other, more conservative countries see consumerism as a threat to their traditional culture. A few leaders have tried to limit Western influence. For example, during the 1990s, there was talk in Zambia about banning imports of Western clothing, but few serious moves have been made in this direction. African TV stations carry adverts for Western products, but little care is taken to adapt the messages for local audiences, many of whom are unused to Western 'marketing-speak', and tend to regard the adverts with scepticism or confusion. One villager, for example, reported his bewilderment at the slogan, 'Coke adds life', when he felt no extra 'life' having drunk a bottle.

Does Consumerism Affect The Environment?

Consumerism has taken a growing toll on the environment. One issue is the waste produced by large-scale manufacturing and consumption. This has contributed to the contamination of rivers, the poisoning of soils and the pollution of air in many towns and cities.

MASSIVE QUANTITIES of rubbish are thrown away each year – an inevitable by-product of the consumer culture. Much of this is non-biodegradable (made of substances that do not break down naturally, such as chemicals, plastics and metals). The developed world is responsible for most of this waste. For example, around 200 billion cans, bottles and plastic cartons get dumped every year in developed countries. The USA alone, with less then five per cent of the world's population, consumes around 30 per cent of the world's energy resources and produces around 19 per cent of the world's

Thousands of tonnes of rubbish are buried each day in landfill sites around the world. Bulldozers compact the waste which is then covered with soil.

In January 2000, 100 000 cubic metres of highly toxic cyanide leaked from a Romanian gold mine into the local river network. Almost all fish and animal life was wiped out on the Tisza river, which flows through Romania and Hungary. Fish were killed as far away as the Danube, several hundred kilometres from the site of the leakage. It will be many years before life on these rivers fully recovers.

The cyanide spill in the Tisza river devastated local wildlife, badly affecting the river's fish as well as protected species such as otters and white-tailed eagles.

domestic waste. Each time a car is driven, it produces carbon dioxide, which pollutes the air. North Americans produce 18 times more carbon dioxide per person than Africans.

How does consumerism lead to pollution?

One reason for the increasing amount of waste is the trend towards 'disposable' items – products designed to be used once before being thrown away. Fragile or edible products usually come with large amounts of packaging, which further adds to waste. The problem is also not helped by the 'planned obsolescence' of products such as computers and mobile phones. Every year, fully functioning products like these get thrown out in favour of the latest models.

Mass consumerism obviously depends on the mass production of goods, and the manufacturing process itself is often a major cause of waste. Much of the waste produced in the manufacturing process is dumped directly into rivers and oceans, or released as gases into the air. Some of this industrial waste is hazardous to human, animal and plant life. Some 80 000 different chemicals are regularly used in modern factories, and many of these chemicals are harmful in themselves, while others produce hazardous wastes during their use. Major rivers, like the Rhine in Western Europe and the Ganges in India, are so polluted from industrial waste that wildlife has disappeared along large stretches of their length.

As well as causing deforestation, livestock farming leads to a loss of topsoil. It has been estimated that for every kilogramme of red meat, poultry, eggs and milk produced, fields lose about 5kg of topsoil.

What is the impact on the rainforests?

Consumer-driven demand for more food at cheaper prices has encouraged large areas of tropical rainforest to be turned over to intensive agriculture. Rainforest soil is less rich than soils in other areas because most of the nutrients are stored in the trees and plants themselves. When the trees are cut down or burned to clear the area for farmland, most of the nutrients disappear with them. The fragile soil is rapidly exhausted through cultivation, forcing farmers to cut down or burn yet more forest, and start all over again. This wasteful method of agriculture is known as 'slash and burn'.

Grazing cattle do a great deal of damage to rainforest areas. In India, nomadic cattle farmers have been forced away from their traditional pastures by the establishment of permanent farms. Their cattle now graze on rainforest margins, destroying much of the plantlife there.

Livestock farming

Intensive livestock breeding for the fast-food industry has had a major environmental impact. Compared to crop farming, livestock farming is also inefficient in terms of the amount of water it uses, because water is necessary to cultivate the crops to feed the cattle and for the cattle to drink.

Of India's 400 million cattle, 90 million live on rainforest land. Cattle have also caused problems for the South American rainforests: in the 1970s and 1980s, Brazilian landowners were given tax incentives to clear massive areas of rainforest in order to raise cattle for the enormous beef market in the USA. However, this policy led to the destruction of so great an area of rainforest that it has now been stopped.

What else damages the rainforests?

Water is plentiful in tropical regions, and governments in these regions often use this resource to generate electricity, by building huge hydro-electric dams. Some of these dams are used to power large-scale industrial processes such as steel production and aluminium smelting. However, building these dams often requires the flooding of large areas of rainforest.

Rainforest land is frequently mined for precious minerals, including silver and gold. Mining operations cause immense damage to the local environment: large areas must be cleared and access roads built; heavy machinery flattens the soil; and local rivers are often polluted by the poisonous substances used in the mining process. For example, in the gold mines of the Amazon in South America, mercury is used to separate gold from gravel. To extract 100 tonnes of gold, at least 130 tonnes of poisonous mercury is released into the environment.

Every day, one in four Americans visits a fast-food restaurant. The mass production of beef to feed this demand has taken a toll on the rainforests.

DEBATE – Are consumers to blame for the destruction of the rainforests?

- Yes. By reducing consumption, there would be no need to destroy so much rainforest land and turn it into farmland.
- No. It is the responsibility of the farmers who slash and burn and the governments that fail to control the situation.

Why Are Some People Opposed To Consumerism?

As we have seen, consumerism has had a major impact on society, human rights and the environment. Most people are happy to go on enjoying its benefits. Some, however, see consumerism as something harmful and dangerous that must be opposed. This has led to the formation of anti-consumerist movements.

Preparing food in a hippy commune in the 1960s.

IN THE 1960s, the hippy movement was made up mostly of young people who rejected the consumerist lifestyle of their parents. They tried to form alternative, non-consumerist communes, which were based on a more natural way of life, in which personal relationships mattered more than possessions. The movement eventually faded and, ironically, certain products of that era, such as colourful clothing and rock music, have become consumer items themselves.

More effective and long-lasting than the hippy movement has been the environmentalist, or green, movement, which began to gather pace in the 1970s.

Environmental groups, such as Greenpeace and Friends of the Earth, have urged governments, businesses and individuals to take more care of the natural world, and consumerism has been a major target of their criticism. Environmentalists have tried to encourage people to think more carefully about how they consume. They have brought attention to the plight of the world's rainforests, the effects of air pollution and many other problems caused by consumerism. The green movement has had only a limited impact on consumerism. However, it has at least been successful in raising awareness of environmental problems.

What is anti-globalisation?

In the late 1990s, a new movement arose protesting against globalisation. This is the trend towards global economic interdependence due to the increasing flow of money around the world. The protestors claim that globalisation has brought wealth and power to large, multinational companies at the expense of ordinary people. Many blame this on the culture of consumerism in the West, which encourages multinationals to continue with their exploitative policies. They argue that the only way to change the behaviour of multinationals is for consumers to stop buying products that are manufactured using methods that harm the environment or exploit people.

Stop buying

'People say if we stop buying so many things, the economy will collapse. I say, we are buying the wrong things. If we buy high-quality, sustainably made goods – even if we buy fewer of them – the economy will be stronger and more stable than ever. Let's face the facts, an economy based on the increasing consumption of resources is only temporary, because the amount of resources on the planet, without a doubt, is finite. Once the Earth is all used up, we don't simply move to the next valley.'

Source: Bob Horowitz, Sustainable Enterprises

Demonstrators march through Washington, DC during an anti-globalisation protest in September 2002.

Religious opposition

Ayatollah Khomeini, who led a religious revolution in Iran in 1979, was a critic of Western consumerism: 'We have nothing to say to those whose powers of perception are so limited that they regard the wearing of European hats, the cast-offs of the wild beasts of Europe, as a sign of national progress.' Khomeini's targets were all those 'who have grown up with lechery, treachery, music and dancing, and a thousand other varieties of corruption... It is a veritable flood of forbidden consumption that sweeps past us, right before our eyes.'

Does consumerism face opposition in non-Western countries?

In non-Western countries, consumerism is often associated with Westernisation – the global spread of Western (mainly American) culture. This can be seen by the appearance of Western fashions, pop music, Hollywood movies, satellite television and McDonald's restaurants in almost every country of the world. In Mexico, for example, the local film industry went from making 100 films in a year to just 10 films in 1998, mainly because of competition from Hollywood. In the remote West Pokot region of Kenya, young people have virtually abandoned traditional dress in favour of trousers and t-shirts.

Consumerism and Westernisation have understandably caused resentment in parts of South America, Africa and Asia, where people fear the loss of their own national or cultural identity. However, there have been few coordinated efforts

The first McDonald's restaurant in Russia opened in Moscow in 1990. It had 700 seats and served 50 000 people a day. Today, there are 58 outlets in cities all over Russia.

In Kenya, Masai tribesmen work as guides, taking Western tourists on safari.

DEBATE – Is there an alternative to globalisation?

- Yes. It is called 'localisation'. People should try to buy their products from local shops and markets, avoid the big brands and support local producers.
- No. Thanks to modern communication technologies and the requirements of multinationals to seek new markets, globalisation is an unstoppable process.

to reject these processes. This is partly because Westernisation has also brought economic benefits to non-Western countries. Tourism, for example, is one kind of consumerism that has helped certain cultures, such as the Masai of Kenya and the Padaung of Myanmar and Thailand, which have been strengthened by the interest of tourists.

What about Islamic countries?

The most significant non-Western anti-consumerist movement is Islamism (a very strict form of Islam), which is a powerful force in many Muslim countries across the Middle East, southern Asia and North Africa.

Islamists regard consumerism as a product of Western decadence, and put pressure on their governments to ban Western products and adverts.

In Iran, consumerism has been denounced by the ruling Islamist Muslim clerics, and, while richer Iranians have been attracted to Western luxuries, many ordinary Iranians see the consumerist attitudes of the West as alien to their culture. Anti-consumerism was a major force behind the revolution in 1979, which brought an Islamist government to power in Iran. One of the first acts of the new government was to insist that women give up their Western clothing and conceal themselves in the traditional 'chador' – a dark garment that covers the head and body.

Consumerism has also been criticised by Islamist movements in Turkey, Algeria and Egypt. For example, in July 2001, conservative religious authorities issued a condemnation of the Egyptian version of the Western gameshow *Who Wants to be a Millionaire*.

Is Consumerism Good Or Bad?

Consumerism is both a positive and a negative force in today's society. It has undeniable environmental, social and cultural costs. Yet consumerism has also contributed to a great improvement in most people's quality of life, and it has helped to break down social division and hierarchy, and given people a sense of global belonging.

The first door-to-door salesmen succeeded in bringing the marketplace into people's own homes.

CONSUMERISM, AS already discussed, has caused significant environmental, social and cultural problems, because of the way that goods are produced and sold around the globe. It also encourages a shallow and materialistic approach to life. It emphasises the importance of buying things over other activities, like exercise, worship, artistic creativity or study. Our energies are focused on satisfying our material desires rather than on developing our minds or our spirits.

What are the negative aspects of consumerism?

Adverts attempt to manipulate us by encouraging needs that never existed before, and by making us more conformist in our choices. This mentality leads us to buy similar products, and in this sense, consumerism can be seen as the enemy of diversity and individualism. It has contributed to a growing sameness in people's lifestyles, desires and aspirations.

Is there a positive side to consumerism?

Consumerism is certainly not all bad. It has contributed to a general rise in people's standard of living. It has encouraged producers to come up with cheaper varieties of products that had previously been enjoyed only by the very rich, and introduced people on lower incomes to luxuries and comforts they could never have otherwise afforded. It has also given a higher profile to consumers as a group, and has given people a sense of their rights to good-quality service from suppliers.

Consumerism does not always mean the imposing of Western styles on other cultures. Despite the power of Western multinational companies, there are plenty of examples of home-grown consumerism in non-Western societies. Japan and India have managed to become consumerist without totally surrendering to Western values. India, for example, now has the world's largest film industry.

Some consumerist products have managed to travel successfully from non-Western to Western countries. For example, Japan has successfully begun to export its own culture to Europe, the United States, the Middle East and other parts of Asia, with products like Pokémon, comic animation, soap operas and computer games. African styles of music and fashion have become popular in the West, and foods, such as curry from India and sushi from Japan, have now become established favourites in the UK.

India has successfully held off American influence by creating its own movie industry.

The Body Shop has led the way in using recycled materials to package and sell its products.

Could consumerism be less costly?

Most of the groups who protest against consumerism accept that they can never defeat it entirely. Society has grown too accustomed to a certain standard of living to give it all up voluntarily. However, there are some things that can be done to curb the most damaging effects of consumerism. Individuals can take more care over how they consume; governments and international agencies can publicise the risks of over-consumption and regulate the exploitative practices of multinationals.

There are various ways in which people can adapt their lives without completely rejecting consumerism, that would be less costly to other people and the planet. They can buy products that do not harm the environment or animals or exploit workers in their manufacture; free-range eggs, for example, or cosmetics that have not been tested on animals. Organic meat is both healthier to the consumer and kinder to animals and the environment, than burgers bought in fast-food restaurants. Ethical consumers can make sure that what they buy was produced by a member of a fair trade organisation, which will ensure that a fair price is paid to farmers.

How can we limit the negative effects?

Consumerism has given society a taste for luxuries – things which are nice, but not strictly necessary. To limit the negative effects of over-consumption, consumers could ask themselves 'What do I need?' rather than 'What do I want?' when they enter a store. In particular, they could limit their use of disposable products, which use up the planet's resources and add to the problem of waste. Clothing and electrical goods can be used until they are worn out, and not thrown away just because a new fashion or model is in the shops. Pollution can be reduced by buying a bicycle, and driving only when necessary. Waste could be cut by turning off a running tap, reusing containers and packaging rather than throwing them away, buying loose fruit and vegetables rather than packaged ones, and buying in bulk.

Governments could also do more to reduce the problems of consumerism. For example, they could encourage industry to develop efficient technologies to deal with waste and pollution, educate children about the costs of consumerism, regulate advertising to children and put pressure on companies to pay fairer wages to workers in developing countries.

DEBATE – Is it realistic to expect everyone to become ethical consumers?

- Yes. The process has already begun, with millions of people recycling their rubbish and eating organic and free-range meat. If new generations are educated about the dangers of over-consumption, then gradually ethical consumerism will become the norm.

- No. Most people love their current lifestyle too much to compromise for the sake of the world at large.

This march, held in Geneva, Switzerland, in June 1998, was against the use of child labour in the production of many goods.

What Is The Future Of Consumerism?

How will consumerism change and develop in the years to come? The culture of consumerism is so ingrained in modern society that we are unlikely to see any dramatic adjustment of lifestyles towards more sustainable consumption.

THE PROCESS OF globalisation looks set to continue, with increasingly similar products and brands available around the globe – albeit with regional variations. Advertising will become ever more sophisticated and far-reaching. But consumerism also faces a number of challenges, such as religious revival in different parts of the world, anti-globalisation protests and increasing gaps between rich and poor.

Will consumerism lead to conflict?

Many religious people have strong doubts about consumerism, because it focuses attention on material gain rather than on spiritual development. With a revival of religious feeling in many parts

Local people in Bhutan, where the conservative Buddhist government has purged the country of foreign cultures and consumerism.

of the world, the conflict between religion and consumerism is likely to continue. This is especially the case with the rise of Islamism in the Muslim world. In the 1990s, the arrival of US military forces in Kuwait led to a growing interest in consumerism among the local people, but the military presence also inspired the hostility of Islamic conservatives, and led to several terrorist incidents.

Strict Christians tend not to be strongly opposed to consumerism in general, and, in fact, many fundamentalist Christian preachers enjoy a wealthy, consumerist lifestyle themselves. They reserve their condemnation for those aspects of consumerism regarded as sinful, such as drinking alcohol, gambling, drug dealing and prostitution. Religious feeling can coexist with consumerism, but not without tensions. For some, religion may provide an alternative to consumerism.

The anti-globalisation movement is still in its early stages, and it is unclear how big it will grow. It is currently weakened by its lack of focus and leadership. But one issue that unites the human rights activists, environmentalists, anti-capitalists and others that make up the movement is concern over consumerism and its effects. All of these groups believe that protecting people's rights and the environment is more important than keeping consumers satisfied. It is unlikely that the anti-globalisation movement will grow strong enough to put consumerism into reverse, but it may be able to place sufficient pressure on companies worried about their public image to make them change their ways.

In 2003, the return of thousands of US and British soldiers to the Middle East saw tensions start to rise again.

Correcting the imbalance

'If the trends continue without change – not redistributing from high-income to low-income consumers, not shifting from polluting to cleaner goods and production technologies, not promoting goods that empower poor producers, not shifting priority from consumption for conspicuous display to meeting basic needs – today's problems of consumption and human development will worsen.'

Anup Shah, *Behind Consumption and Consumerism*, September 2001

Will consumerism make the world more united?

Another shadow hanging over consumerism is the gap between rich and poor, which has steadily widened over the past 20 years. Consumerism has left behind vast portions of Africa, and even many people living in the developed West. Currently, the richest fifth of the world's population consume 45 per cent of all meat and fish, 58 per cent of the world's energy and use 87 per cent of the world's vehicles. Whether this huge inequality can be sustained is open to question. It may well lead to new forms of protest.

Even a traditionally Buddhist country such as Japan, has adopted the consumer-led frenzy that Christmas has now become.

What will help to spread consumerism?

Despite these question marks, the likelihood is that consumerism will continue to spread, as more people around the world seek to define themselves, at least in part, by the things they buy. India, Turkey, Mexico and Brazil have sizeable middle classes that already enjoy a consumerist lifestyle. China and Russia are not far behind in their consumerist aspirations.

Globalisation will help this process forward. Young people all over the world, from Manchester to Manila in the Philippines, are already wearing the same styles of dress, listening to the same kinds of music and supporting the same football teams. This sense of a global consumerist culture, especially in the world's cities, is likely to intensify over the coming years, for a number of reasons. First, the communications media is increasingly international in scope, with a small number of giant

Neuromarketing

In the future, consumers may find that companies are well informed about what they want to buy. A new tool is available which may allow companies to map the consumer's mind while they are shopping. Neuromarketing, as this process is called, was developed by a company in Atlanta, USA. It involves scanning people's brains to try and record their thoughts and feelings as they look at pictures of products and adverts. The aim is to bridge the gap between what consumers want and what they actually find on the shelves of their store. Technology such as this can only strengthen consumerism in times to come.

corporations dominating the world's television networks, music, films, newspapers and magazines.

Second, the Internet will give unprecedented numbers of people access to the very latest in popular culture, accelerating the spread of new consumerist trends around the globe. Third, English – the language of around 80 per cent of Internet sites – will be learned and spoken by ever increasing numbers of people. Already, almost one in ten people around the world speak English, and this trend can only help the spread of a global consumerist culture.

For all its faults, consumerism is certainly here to stay. Regulating it is a challenge to be faced by everyone, from global organisations to individuals. Consumerism is clearly a part of human nature, and, ultimately, it should serve the needs of all humans and not place itself in conflict with nature.

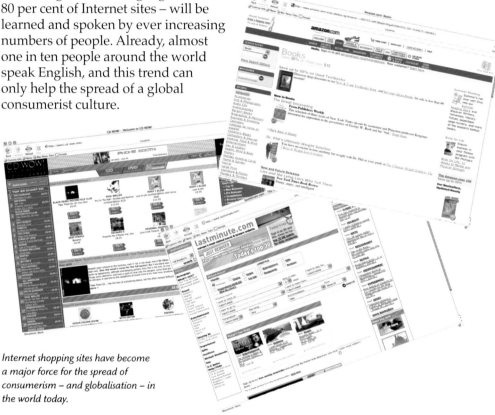

Internet shopping sites have become a major force for the spread of consumerism – and globalisation – in the world today.

DEBATE - Will consumerism continue to grow at the same pace?

- Yes. There are vast markets of potential consumers still to be tapped, in Russia and China, for example.

- No. The current pace of consumerism is unsustainable. It has already met concerted resistance from groups such as environmentalists, anti-capitalists and Islamists, and is likely to meet even greater opposition in the future.

REFERENCE

STATISTICS OF INEQUALITY

THE WORLD'S RICHEST FIFTH:
account for 86 per cent of total private consumption expenditures;
consume 45 per cent of all meat and fish;
consume 58 per cent of total energy;
have 74 per cent of all telephone lines;
consume 84 per cent of all paper;
own some 87 per cent of the world's vehicle fleet.

THE WORLD'S POOREST FIFTH:
account for 1.3 per cent of total private consumption expenditures;
consume 5 per cent of all meat and fish;
consume 4 per cent of total energy;
have 1.5 per cent of all telephone lines;
consume 1.1 per cent of all paper;
own less than one per cent of the world's vehicle fleet.

Source: *Human Development Report 1998 Overview*, United Nations Development Programme

CONSUMPTION

EXPENDITURE ON PRIVATE CONSUMPTION BY COUNTRY IN 2001

Country	£ (in millions)	Country	£ (in millions)
USA	4 206 818	Argentina	112 719
Japan	1 548 791	Poland	69 523
Germany	661 399	Turkey	63 373
UK	559 723	Indonesia	58 083
France	544 215	Hong Kong	57 223
Italy	392 522	Denmark	47 459
China	330 942	South Africa	45 502
Mexico	255 714	Israel	39 645
Canada	223 746	Egypt	38 852
Brazil	211 609	Saudi Arabia	33 179
India	154 570	Algeria	14 995
Russia	154 525	Nigeria	14 964
Australia	130 056		

Source: *Euromonitor International, 2002*

CONSUMPTION

WORLD CONSUMPTION OF CONSUMER PRODUCTS IN 2001

Product	£ (in millions)	percentage of total expenditure
Clothing and footwear	8812	6.16
Cars	7770	5.43
Furniture	4343	3.03
Meat	3458	2.42
Alcoholic drinks	2240	1.56
Household appliances	1403	0.98
Confectionery	1283	0.90
Glassware and tableware	856	0.60
Fish	653	0.46
Air travel	596	0.42
Carpets	592	0.41
Coffee, tea and cocoa	578	0.40

Source: *Euromonitor International*, 2002

CORPORATIONS

CORPORATIONS COMPARED WITH COUNTRIES IN 1999

Corporation or Country	Sales or Gross Domestic Product (GDP) (US$ billion)
General Motors	176.6
Denmark	176.0
Ford Motor Company	162.6
Exxon Mobil Corporation	160.9
Wal-Mart Stores	137.6
South Africa	130.2
Israel	100.8
Malaysia	79.0
Sony Corporation	63.1
McDonald's Corporation	13.3
Jamaica	7.2

Sources: UNCTAD and World Bank

ADVERTISING

GLOBAL ADVERTISING EXPENDITURE (US$ BILLIONS)

Category	2002	2003	% rise	% of share
TV	126.5	134	6	51.1
Press	98.1	100.3	2.6	38.3
Radio	11.1	11.5	3.7	4.4
Outdoor	10.3	10.9	2.2	4.2
Internet	4.1	4.3	4.1	1.6
Cinema	0.9	1	10.6	0.4
Total	251	262		100

Source: Responservice, 2003

TOTAL EXPENDITURE ON ADVERTISING IN THE UK IN 2000

Category	£ millions
Retail and mail order	995
Financial	805
Cars	734
Food	596
Entertainment and media	504
Industrial	462
Office equipment	418
Toiletries and cosmetics	369
Leisure equipment	331
Drink	284
Travel and transport	282
Household stores	219
Pharmaceutical	190
Government, charity and educational	160
Clothing	152

Source: The Advertising Association

THE ENVIRONMENT

SOLID WASTE DISPOSAL METHODS AS A PERCENTAGE OF TOTAL

Country	Landfill	Incineration	Recycling/Composting
Japan	27	69	4
Korea	72	4	24
Denmark	22	54	24
Sweden	39	42	19
UK	84	9	7
Switzerland	14	46	40
USA	57	16	27
Mexico	99	0	1
Canada	75	6	19
Greece	93	0	7
France	59	32	9

Source: Organisation for Economic Cooperation and Development (OECD), 1995

THREATS TO TROPICAL RAINFORESTS

Region	Original forest under threat (%)	Threats to forest (%)				
		Logging	Mining, roads, etc	Cleared for agriculture	Cleared for other uses	Other causes*
Africa	77	79	12	17	8	41
Asia	60	50	10	20	9	24
S. America	54	69	53	32	14	5
World	39	72	38	20	14	13

* Other causes includes plantations, fire and the splitting of forests into smaller fragments.
NB: The percentage risks add up to more than 100 per cent since forests may be threatened by more than one factor.

Source: *21st Century Debates: Rainforests*, Ewan McLeish, Hodder Wayland 2001

CARBON DIOXIDE EMISSIONS

Region	Metric tons per person
North America	19.9
Oceania	11.3
Europe and Russia	8.5
Central America	3.6
South America	2.4
Asia	2.3
Africa	1.1

Source: *1998–99 World Resources Report*

GLOSSARY

capitalism An economic system characterised by a free competitive market and based on private ownership of the means of production.

carbon dioxide A heavy, colourless, odourless atmospheric gas. It is formed by combustion, and increasing levels of this gas in the atmosphere may be responsible for altering the Earth's temperature and weather patterns.

cardiovascular Relating to the heart and blood vessels.

cash crop A crop grown for sale rather than personal consumption.

Christian fundamentalism A strict form of Christianity based on a literal interpretation of the Bible.

class A group of people within a society who share a similar social and economic status.

coca A yellow-flowered shrub, native to the Andes mountains in South America, whose leaves yield cocaine.

cocaine An illegal drug obtained from the leaves of the coca plant.

colony An overseas territory ruled by another country.

commodity An item that is bought and sold.

communism A system, or the belief in a system, in which capitalism is overthrown and the state controls wealth and property.

conspicuous Attracting attention through being unusual or remarkable.

cosmetic surgery Surgery carried out on the body intended to improve a person's physical appearance.

decadent Behaving in an immoral way.

deforestation The clearing of trees from a forest.

developed countries The wealthy and technologically advanced countries of the world.

disposable Designed to be thrown away after use.

electorate The group of people who are able to vote in an election.

endorsement The official approval by a person, organisation or cartoon character of a product.

Enlightenment An 18th-century movement in Western Europe that emphasised the use of reason and science in human life and culture.

environmentalism A movement that works towards protecting the natural world from harmful human activities.

free-range A term that refers to farm animals, and means that they are free to move around and feed at will, rather than being confined in a battery or pen.

globalisation The trend towards global economic interdependence due to the increasing flow of money and investments by big businesses around the world.

Islam The religion of Muslims, based on the teachings of the seventh-century prophet Muhammad.

Islamism A strict form of Islam based on a literal interpretation of the Qur'an and other holy Islamic scriptures.

kosher Food that has been prepared in a way that complies with Jewish law.

localisation A way of living in which people buy their goods and services from local markets and suppliers to create stronger local economies.

loom A hand-operated or machine-operated device for weaving cloth.

malnutrition A lack of healthy foods in the diet, or an excessive intake of unhealthy foods, leading to physical harm and diseases.

mercury A poisonous, heavy, silver-white metallic chemical that is used in some industrial processes.

multinational company A large company that operates or has investments in several different countries throughout the world.

nomadic Referring to tribes or groups of people who move from place to place seasonally in search of pasture for their herds, or in search of food and water.

obesity A condition in which somebody's weight is 20 per cent higher than that which is recommended for that person's height and body type.

obsolescence When an object is replaced by something new.

organic Food that has been grown or reared without the use of too many synthetic chemicals, such as pesticides, hormones or fertilisers.

rainforest A thick, evergreen, tropical forest found in areas of heavy rainfall and containing trees with broad leaves that form a continuous canopy (covering) over the ground.

recession A period of decline in economic trade and prosperity.

retail The selling of goods in small amounts directly to customers, especially in shops.

smelting Melting ore in order to get metal from it.

software Programmes or applications that can be run on a computer.

Soviet Union Also known as the USSR (Union of Soviet Socialist Republics), it was a country formed in 1917 from the territories of the Russian Empire. It lasted until 1991.

sponsor A person or organisation who provides money to help fund something such as an institution, a sports career, a TV programme or a particular event, usually in return for publicity.

sushi Small cakes of cold boiled rice, shaped by hand or wrapped in seaweed and topped with pieces of raw or cooked fish, vegetables or egg.

tax incentive An offer to reduce tax to encourage a company or individual to act in a certain way.

therapy Treatment of mental or behavioural problems that is meant to cure or rehabilitate someone.

topsoil The upper, fertile layer of soil, from which plant roots take nutrients.

FURTHER INFORMATION

BOOKS

Consumerism in World History,
Peter N Stearns, Routledge 2001
Consumerism Issues, Craig Donnellan
(ed.), Independence 1999
Consumerism as a Way of Life, Steve Miles,
Sage Publications 1998
21st Century Debates: Globalisation,
Rob Bowden, Hodder Wayland 2003
21st Century Debates: Rainforests,
Ewan McLeish, Hodder Wayland 2001
Mediawise: Advertising, Julian Petley,
Hodder Wayland 2002
Life Files: Food Matters, Jillian Powell,
Evans Brothers 1999
Sustainable Future: Business and Industry,
Simon Beavis and Chris Barrie,
Franklin Watts 2002
*What do we mean about human rights:
Workers' Rights*, Katherine Prior,
Franklin Watts 2002
Viewpoints: A Green World, Nicola Baird,
Franklin Watts 2001

VIDEOS

All the Right Stuff (23 minutes),
Dir: Connie Littlefield, The National
Film Board of Canada 1998
Teaches young consumers about media,
malls, money and consumerism.

The Bomb under the World (52 minutes),
Dir: Werner Volkmer, Green Lion
Productions 1995
What are the consequences of
consumerism taking hold in developing
countries like India?

WEBSITES

http://www.newdream.org
A website containing suggestions for
how to combat the negative effects of
consumerism.

**http://cmb.physics.wisc.edu/~friess/
consumer**
Socially conscious consumerism.
A website with links to non-exploitative
retailers.

**http://www.media-awareness.ca/
english/parents/marketing/index.cfm**
A webpage from a Canadian website
called Media Awareness Network,
which looks at the issues of marketing,
advertising and consumerism,
particularly as they relate to children.

http://www.wastewatch.org.uk
A website containing information about
waste, recycling and reuse.

http://www.rainforests.net
A website with the latest information
about rainforest clearance and other
related issues.

**http://www.globalmarch.org/
child_labour_today**
The website of Global March against
Child Labour, which gives facts and case
studies about child labour in several
developing nations.

The following website is very anti-consumerist, full of facts and opinions about the negative effects of consumerism and suggestions for how to defeat consumerism:
http://www.globalissues.org/ TradeRelated/Consumption.asp

If you want to read an essay in praise of consumerism, try:
http://reason.com/0008/fe.jt.in.shtml

ORGANISATIONS

Fair Trade Federation
1612 K Street NW, Suite 600,
Washington, DC 20006
Tel: +1 800 584 7336
http://www.fairtradefederation.com/
An association of fair trade wholesalers, retailers and producers whose members are committed to providing fair wages and good employment opportunities to poor craftspeople and farmers around the world.

The Fairtrade Foundation
Suite 204, 16 Baldwin's Gardens,
London EC1N 7RJ
Tel: 020 7405 5942
http://www.fairtrade.org.uk/
The Fairtrade Foundation exists to promote a better deal for producers in poorer countries. The foundation awards the 'Fairtrade' mark to products who meet internationally recognised standards of fair trade.

Oxfam
Oxfam House
274 Banbury Road
Oxford
OX2 7DZ
Tel: 01865 312610

Friends of the Earth
26–28 Underwood Street
London N1 7QJ
Tel: 020 7490 1555
http://www.foe.co.uk

Greenpeace Environmental Trust
Canonbury Villas
London N1 2PN
Tel: 020 7865 8100
http://www.greenpeace.org.uk

INDEX